cat treats

cat treats

fun • facts • food

Janice Anderson

hamlyn

First published in Great Britain in 2002 by Hamlyn, a division of
Octopus Publishing Group Ltd, 2–4 Heron Quays, London E14 4JP

ISBN 0 600 60719 4

A CIP catalogue record for this book is available from the British Library

Printed and bound in China

10 9 8 7 6 5 4 3 2 1

Notes for American readers

Both metric and imperial measurements have been used in all recipes. Use one set
of measurements only, and not a mixture of both.

Standard level spoon measurements are used in all recipes.
1 tablespoon = one 15 ml spoon
1 teaspoon = one 5 ml spoon

Ovens should be preheated to the specified temperature – if using a fan-assisted
oven, follow the manufacturer's instructions for adjusting the time and
temperature.

UK	US
double cream	heavy cream
grilled	broiled
minced beef	ground beef
prawns	shrimp
single cream	light or coffee cream
wholemeal	wholewheat

what's inside

- ## Tasty tidbits
  30 simple recipes – healthy, whisker-licking fare for everyday and special occasions

  Plus............

- **cats and us** Cat myths and legends from around the world

- **understanding your cat** How to read feline body language and communicate with your puss

- **artistic cats** Best-selling cats on canvas

- **celebrity cats** Cats with celebrity status

- **kitty quotations** Proverbs and who said what about our purring friends

- **pussycats in print** Poems, prose and literary connections

- **state cats** World leaders with a passion for cats

- **guiding paws** Cats that inspired some of the most famous writers of our time

- **funny felines** Amusing catty quips and quotes

- **cat stars** Past and present idols of the silver screen

- **alley cats and pedigrees** A look at the characteristics of common, posh and quirky cats

- **cat statistics** Facts about cats past, present and fictional

introduction

Cats will eat any food common to their environment. Italian cats are adept at dealing with spaghetti while cats in Australia enjoy a small snake, or half a snake – it doesn't matter which half! – after the haymower has gone through. In fact, the consensus among cat lovers Down Under is that antipodean cats don't have special treats – they are humans in fur clothes and happily partake of all human food.

spicing up your cat's diet
Cats living in big cities may well envy their free-ranging Australian cousins. For most domestic cats, food comes out of a can or a carton. The pet food industry in the West, worth billions of dollars each year, may be based on producing food that is carefully balanced to provide the cat's full nutritional needs, but even the best of it must become boring after a while. In addition, cats fed solely on manufactured foods often get fat because their owners unwittingly give them too much.

healthy home-made fare
Experts consider that an ideal weight for the average cat, whether a moggy or a pedigree, is about 3.5–5.8 kg (8–12½ lb). Big cats, like the Maine Coon, can be perfectly healthy

weighing as much as 10 kg (22 lb). If your cat is getting too heavy for you to pick up, then there is all the more reason to feed him from this book. Not only are these recipes great treats for cats, they are also based on good cat nutrition. The majority of them are suggested in amounts that will provide one or two good meals, depending on the size of your cat.

There are 'special' ingredients in some recipes, including brewer's yeast and bonemeal. Available from pet stores or healthfood suppliers, these provide extra vitamins, minerals and fibre. Although cats need some salt in the diet, they do not need very much, so be sparing with it and use iodized salt, for its iodine content, if possible. Cats will get extra, valuable vitamins from fresh parsley and watercress sprinkled over food, and from a few drops of cod liver oil.

the great flood

Noah did not let mice on board the Ark: the Devil put them there so they could nibble a hole in it and sink it. Noah asked Lion for help and Lion snorted out of his nostrils two cats – one male and one female. It is a good story, even though a popular explanation of how the Manx cat lost his tail contradicts it. The cat was slow in reaching the Ark and Noah had already battened down the hatches, only agreeing to open one again if the cat would agree to catch the mice on board. The cat said yes, but was again a bit slow so that the hatch came down on his tail, chopping it off.

manx cats

A Manx cat can be a 'rumpy' (completely tailless), a 'rumpy riser' (with one, two or three vertebrae fused to the spine and making a tiny knob), a 'stumpy' or 'stubby' (with a short but movable tail stump), or a 'longy' (with an almost full-length tail).

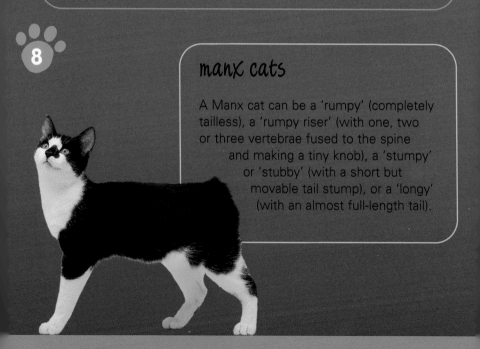

feline fare

This tangy mixture is lip-licking tasty and wonderfully nutritious. Once cooked, it can be kept in the fridge for three to four days. It also freezes well, provided you have used fresh, not previously frozen, fish and liver.

250 g/8 oz lamb or pig's liver
250 g/8 oz piece of white fish
50 g/2 oz/½ cup dry cat food
125 ml/4 fl oz/½ cup tomato juice
½ teaspoon cod liver oil

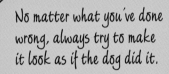

No matter what you've done wrong, always try to make it look as if the dog did it.

Cat's motto

1 Put the liver and fish in a pan with water to cover and simmer gently until cooked, about 8–10 minutes. Meanwhile, soak the dry cat food in the tomato juice.
2 Drain the cooked liver and fish, setting aside the cooking liquid. Flake the fish, carefully removing all the bones.
3 Put the liver, fish, soaked cat food and cod liver oil in a blender or food processor and process in short bursts, so that the mixture does not become too creamy. Use the cooking liquid to adjust the consistency to your cat's liking.

!**tip**

**Do not feed
your cat raw egg
white: it contains a
chemical that can
destroy important
vitamins.**

the cat in scottish heraldry

Defeated in his attempt to stop Moses
and the Israelites crossing the parted
waters of the Red Sea, the Greek general
Galsthelos, commander of the Egyptian
Pharaoh's army, finally settled in Portugal
with his beautiful wife, Scota, the
Pharaoh's daughter. Centuries later a
descendant, Fergus I, founded a nation
far to the north which he named Scotia,
after his Egyptian ancestress. Perhaps
remembering Bastet, the cat-headed
goddess of ancient Egypt, Fergus chose
as his new country's emblem a cat. The
cat and its splendid cousin, the lion, are
prominent in the national, clan and family
heraldry of Scotland to this day.

prophet's cat

state cats

Muezza, favourite cat of Mohammed,
once went to sleep on the sleeve of
the Prophet's robe and Mohammed,
called to prayer, chose to cut the sleeve
off his robe rather than disturb his cat.

scrummy scrambled treat

This is a quickly made treat for those times when your cat deserves something special. The protein in eggs makes them good for cats, although two to three servings a week are enough.

1 teaspoon butter
1 egg, lightly beaten with a little water
1 teaspoon finely chopped fresh parsley
1 cabbage or spring greens leaf, finely
   chopped (optional)
25 g/1 oz/¼ cup dry cat food

1 Melt the butter gently in a small pan, pour in the egg and whisk it until it is scrambled.
2 Take the pan off the heat and stir in the parsley, greens, if using, and the dry cat food.

cat stars

Cat actor Orangey played Rhubarb, an alley cat who inherited a fortune and a baseball team in 'Rhubarb' (1951).

a london myth

The story of Dick Whittington and his cat is one of the best known of England's cat stories. The story goes that Dick Whittington was a poor but honest orphan trying to stay alive in a city where, contrary to legend, the streets were not paved with gold. He got work in the mice-infested kitchens of a rich merchant and bought for one penny a splendid cat that was so good at killing mice that the merchant took it from Dick and put it on mice-catching duty on one of his trading ships bound for the Barbary coast. Discouraged by the loss of his cat, Dick made to leave London, but was stopped on Highgate Hill by the pealing of the bells of Bow, which seemed to be calling 'Turn again, Whittington, thrice Mayor of London'. Dick returned to London, subsequently making his fortune from the sale of his cat to a Moorish ruler whose court was over-run by rats. Dick married well and eventually had three turns as Lord Mayor of London, followed by a period as a Member of Parliament.

fact or fiction?

There is some truth in all this. Sir Richard Whittington was indeed Lord Mayor of London three times and a Member of Parliament at the turn of the 14th century.

And he was an immensely rich merchant, supplying expensive textiles and fabrics to the royal court and the nobility. But he was not a poor orphan and he probably never had a cat. It is thought that his success owed much to the fact that he paid bribes or 'favours', called achats (pronounced a-cat), something which a popular ballad of the time may have been referring to in describing 'how his rise was by a cat'.

An alternative explanation derives from the term 'cat' or 'catch' for a style of ship used in the coal trade. According to tradition, Sir Richard Whittington made his money by trading in coals, which he conveyed in his 'cat'. The blackened faces of his coalmen account for the tale about the Moors.

set in stone

A bronze statue of Dick Whittington's cat rests on the Whittington Stone on Highgate Hill in north London. The stone is said to be the one on which Dick rested on his way out of London in about 1390.

fishy wishes

tip

Never give a cat food straight from the fridge. Cats like food when it is 'mouse temperature' – that is, warm on the tongue.

14

A pâté as a starter or a party snack for your cats? Why not – cats are as likely to be as discerning about their food as you are!

250 g/8 oz piece of smoked white fish fillet
15 g/½ oz/1 tablespoon butter, softened
1 teaspoon brewer's yeast
½ teaspoon finely chopped fresh parsley
toast, to serve

1 Put the fish in a baking dish or saucepan, pour over boiling water, cover and set aside for 10 minutes.

2 Lift the fish out of the water, draining it well. Skin and flake the fish, removing any bones that may have been left in the fillet. Put the flaked fish in a bowl, add the butter and mash together to make a spreadable mixture. Mix in the brewer's yeast and parsley.

3 To serve the pâté, spread some of it on a slice of toast and cut into small bite-sized squares or fish shapes. (Any leftover pâté can be stored, covered, in the fridge, but bring it to room temperature before serving it to your cat.)

cats in ancient egypt

It is known that the cat has had a place in the world of men for at least 4,500 years, thanks to the careful drawing of a cat with a wide collar around its neck found in an Egyptian tomb dating back to the Fifth Dynasty (*c*.2600 BC).

The Egyptian Mau, a very handsome cat, has been bred to be as similar as possible to the cat of ancient Egypt. Cats were so revered in those days that when a household cat died, its owners shaved off their eyebrows as a sign of mourning and performed serious funeral rites that included embalming the cat and burying it in a necropolis dedicated solely to cats.

biblical cats

The domestic cat is not mentioned in the Old Testament, perhaps because the Jews, freed from slavery in Egypt, wished to have nothing more to do with the Egyptian culture.

cat talk

Researchers have detected at least 16 separate sounds made by cats when they talk. Apart from the usual cacophony of growls, grumbles, yowls and hisses they emit to inspire fear in something that is causing them stress, cats also use specific sounds to express different needs. Forget about 'miaow' – that's for kittens. Big cats complain by uttering 'mhgn-a-ou'; express surprise with 'maou'; and say 'mhrn-a-ou' when they have something to ask us.

According to zoologist and cat expert Desmond Morris, the cat has two vocabularies. It retains the sound signals that wild kittens use for mother–offspring communication and also acquires others, which it uses for communicating with us and other felines, as it grows to adulthood. The domestic cat, when it goes out into the night, can hurl twice as many calls into the moonlight as its wild cousins, the big cats.

Cats are a mysterious kind of folk. There is more passing in their minds than we are aware of.

Sir Walter Scott, novelist and poet (1771–1832)

cheesy tuna treasure

This mixture of tuna and cheese, with its great protein, vitamin and calcium content, is sure to set your cat purring vigorously.

100 g/3½ oz can tuna in oil or spring water
25 g/1 oz Parmesan, Cheddar or other hard
   cheese, crumbled

1 Drain the can of tuna.
2 Flake the tuna with a fork, removing any visible bones. Pile it on to a heatproof plate. Sprinkle the cheese on top and place under a hot grill until the cheese has begun to melt, but is not too hot.

guiding paws

catarina

Poet, critic and writer, Edgar Allen Poe (1809–1849) worked best with a cat sitting on his shoulder. When Poe was very poor Catarina, the most beloved of his cats, helped his wife, who had consumption, keep warm. Poe was inspired by Catarina's faithfulness to write his best-known story, 'The Black Cat'.

tibbles' nibbles

These crunchy snacks are a cat's
equivalent of our healthfood
cereal bars.

50 g/2 oz raw beef, lamb or chicken, minced
150 g/5 oz/1 cup wholemeal flour
2 tablespoons wheatgerm
2 garlic cloves, crushed
15 g/½ oz/1 tablespoon butter
2 tablespoons black treacle
300 ml/½ pint/1¼ cups beef
   or chicken stock

18

1 Mix together the meat, flour, wheatgerm and garlic. Rub in the butter with your fingertips. Stir in the treacle, then about three-quarters of the stock.

2 Knead the mixture to form a firm dough, adding the remaining stock, if necessary. Roll out on a lightly floured surface to a thickness of about 3 cm/1¼ inches. Cut into squares, and place on a lightly greased baking sheet.

3 Bake in a preheated oven, 180°C/350°F/Gas Mark 4, for about 20 minutes, then turn the squares over and return to the oven for about 15 minutes more. Cool on a wire rack, then store in an airtight container. Break the squares into bite-sized pieces before putting them in your cat's bowl.

cat's eyes

- Cats don't live in an entirely monochrome world. The cat's eye contains two kinds of cone, sensitive to green and blue, but not to red (unlike humans who have three kinds of cone in their eyes). A cat, after much training, can distinguish between red and blue objects and between these two colours and white. Green, yellow and white probably look much the same to a cat, while red looks dark grey.
- Cats cannot see well in full darkness, but they can see well in much dimmer light than we can.
- Because the average adult cat sleeps 16–18 hours a day, its eyes are in fact shut most of the time!
- Cats' eyes glow in the dark because light passing through the eye is not absorbed by the retina. Rather, it strikes a special layer of iridescent cells called the *tapidum lucidum*, which creates the glow.

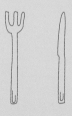

state cats

nelson

A black cat called Nelson helped the war effort in Britain during World War II. He slept on the bed of the Prime Minister acting as a hot-water bottle and thus saving fuel.

!tip

Do not give cats cooked chicken bones. Cooking hardens the bones so that they splinter easily and can be harmful. The cooked bones of larger pieces of meat, such as beef, are safe.

whisker-licking chicken

If several cats live in your house, you need to think big when it comes to food. Here is a great way using a whole chicken.

1 medium chicken
2 carrots
a few Brussels sprouts
handful of fresh herbs (such as parsley, basil, coriander)
salt

1 Put the chicken in a casserole dish. Add the vegetables and herbs and sprinkle over a little salt. Pour in sufficient water to come halfway up the chicken. Cover the casserole.
2 Cook in a preheated oven – about 150°C/300°F/Gas Mark 2. Depending on its size, the chicken should be thoroughly cooked after 2–2½ hours.
3 Remove the chicken from the casserole and set aside to cool. Take the vegetables out of the cooking liquid, chop them up and set aside. Strain the cooking liquid and keep it to use as stock.
4 Give your cats the chicken meat chopped or minced, with some of the chopped vegetables and a little cooking liquid poured over.

the cat's whiskers

Is your cat feeling at ease? Look at his whiskers; if they are set sideways and pointing back, then he is relaxed. When a cat is alert, the whiskers extend forwards as it puffs out its whisker pads. A cat's whiskers are one of three sets of pressure-sensitive hairs, called vibrissae, on its body. The other vibrissae are its eyebrows and the long hairs underneath its front paws.

The cat's whiskers are essential tools in its night-time hunting. They are very sensitive feelers, able to detect the slightest movement of currents in the air. A cat moving in darkness may not see solid objects near it, but its whiskers will pick up the smallest eddy of air caused by its approach to the object, thus enabling it to move around the object without touching it. The whiskers also help the cat to judge exactly where to bite its prey to make a clean kill.

cat stars

Cat, played by the same professional cat actor, Orangey, who played Rhubarb, helped Audrey Hepburn through her troubles in 'Breakfast at Tiffany's' (1961).

bosscat's breakfast

Next time you are cooking liver and bacon for breakfast, prepare enough for your cat, who will not forget this three-star treat in a hurry.

freshly cooked lamb's liver, chopped
1–2 slices of grilled bacon, rinds left on, chopped
a little hard cheese

1 Put the liver and bacon, while still warm, in your cat's bowl and crumble some hard cheese on top. Serve at once.

!tip

Because liver contains lots of vitamin A and cholesterol, which a cat needs, but not in large amounts, it is best to give liver to your cat only about twice a week.

state cats *in japan*

A tenth-century Emperor of Japan, Ichijo, had a cat called Myobu No Omoto whom the Emperor adored so much that when the cat was chased by a dog, the dog was banished and its unfortunate owner imprisoned.

tell-tale tails

A typical cat has 21–23 bones in its tail. Among the advantages to having a long, flexible tail is the ability to semaphore all kinds of messages with it. For example:

- A male cat holding its tail bent forward over its head is signalling 'I am top cat around here'.
- A quivering tail tip indicates excitement; if the tail tip twitches, the cat is saying 'I am starting to get angry'.
- A tail being lashed to and fro is a sign of real anger.
- A tail waved quietly from side to side shows contentment.
- A stiff quick upwards flick of the tail is a greeting signal.

There are seven kinds of domestic cat with short or no tails: the Manx (see page 8); the Cymric, a long-haired version of the Manx; the Japanese Bobtail, which has a tail that is both short and tightly twisted; the Japanese Bobtail Longhair; the Karelian Bobtail; the American Bobtail; and a recent breed, the American Lynx.

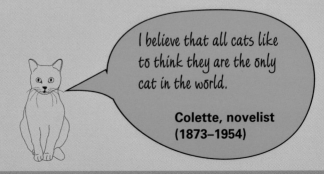

I believe that all cats like to think they are the only cat in the world.

Colette, novelist (1873–1954)

purrfect health

This recipe is adapted from a suggestion for a well-balanced home-made meal in international cat expert Dr Bruce Fogle's book *Natural Cat Care* (Dorling Kindersley, 1999). It makes enough to feed an average-size cat (about 3.5 kg/8 lb) for three days.

65 g/2½ oz/⅛ cup rice
15 g/½ oz bonemeal
1 teaspoon salt
½ teaspoon sunflower or corn oil
150 g/5 oz chicken meat
325 g/11 oz liver

24

1 Put the rice, bonemeal, salt and oil in a heavy-based saucepan. Pour in twice the volume of water. Cover, bring the pan to the boil and simmer for 20 minutes. Add the chicken and liver and simmer for another 10 minutes.
2 Cool the mixture slightly, then pour into a blender or food processor and blend thoroughly so that your cat cannot pick the meat out from the rice.

pounce on 'em prawns

Peeled prawns are a favourite with most cats. This recipe for prawn cocktail turns them into the equivalent of a smart dinner party first course.

75 g/3 oz cooked peeled prawns
a few sprigs of watercress, chopped
2–3 teaspoons plain yogurt
1 slice of wholemeal toast (optional)

1 If the prawns are small, leave them whole; chop them coarsely if large. Put them in a bowl, add the watercress and yogurt and mix well together.
2 Serve the prawn cocktail as it is or, if your cat likes toast, spread it on wholemeal toast cut into bite-sized pieces.

!tip

Watercress is great for cats. It helps tone the circulation and is a good source of vitamins A, B, D and E, and iron.

going veggie?

The cat experts' answer to feeding a cat a vegetarian diet is 'Don't do it!' According to Dr Bruce Fogle: 'It is unnatural, unbalanced and potentially deadly to feed a cat a vegetarian diet.'

purrfect pressies

Lovingly made presents to mark special days in your cat's life mean so much more than shop-bought toys and playthings. Fabric sausage or square shapes, fish or mice stuffed with catnip are easily made and most acceptable. Always choose natural fabrics such as cotton, linen or velvet as cats can become very enthusiastic when playing with catnip-stuffed toys and may inadvertently eat the fabric.

Sausage: The easiest shape for stuffing with catnip and/or other herbs, is a sausage. Cut a rectangle of fabric about 15 x 12.5 cm/ 6 x 5 inches, fold it in half with the right sides facing and sew the long raw edges and one short edge together. Turn the sausage right side out, stuff with catnip, and sew up the remaining short side.

Fish and mice: Fabric mice or fish stuffed with catnip do not need to be very big – a finished size of about 10 cm/4 inches long is fine. Draw the shapes you want to make on plain paper, allowing extra for seams and making your shapes almost as wide as they are long – you want a nicely rounded mouse or fish when it is stuffed. Cut out two pieces of each shape, place them together, with the right sides facing, and sew around the shapes, leaving a small opening unstitched. Turn the fabric right side out, stuff with catnip and sew up the remaining seam.

Playbags: Playbags stuffed with catnip and aromatic herbs will keep cats happy for hours – and they can sleep on them, too. Ideally, these should have a herb-stuffed 'cushion' inside, made from strong cotton such as curtain lining, and an outer bag made of something soft and comfortable like cotton velvet, such as is used for making curtains.

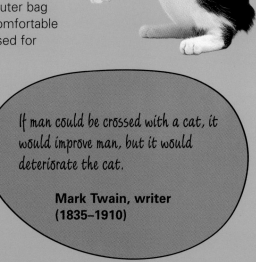

If man could be crossed with a cat, it would improve man, but it would deteriorate the cat.

Mark Twain, writer (1835–1910)

cats on canvas and paper

- Three top-selling reproductions of works in Tate Britain, London, involve cats. They are William Hogarth's *The Graham Children*, David Hockney's *Mr and Mrs Clark and Percy* and Gwen John's watercolour, *Cat*.
- One of the earliest-known depictions of a cat on paper is a lean and spotted animal, the Sun God Ra in cat form, in an Egyptian papyrus version of *The Book of the Dead*, which is 3,200 years old.
- Royal Academician Ruskin Spear painted his cat Oliver in *Cat and Piano*, exhibited at the Royal Academy's 1984 Summer Exhibition in London.
- A page from one of Leonardo da Vinci's sketchbooks crammed with cat drawings is one of the best-known works of cat art of the Renaissance period.

cat stars

Solomon, an outstandingly beautiful Chinchilla, played the villain's pampered pet in two James Bond films, 'You Only Live Twice' (1967) and 'Diamonds are Forever' (1971).

pedigree kedgeree

Meals like this kedgeree
variation keep pedigrees and
moggies alike fit and healthy.

50 g/2 oz/generous ¼ cup rice
1 tablespoon sunflower or corn oil
½ teaspoon mild curry paste (optional)
25 g/1 oz cooked fresh white fish, flaked
   and bones removed
25 g/1 oz cooked smoked white fish, flaked
   and bones removed
knob of butter
1 tablespoon single cream
a little chopped fresh parsley
1 tablespoon chopped hard-boiled egg

1 Cook the rice in lightly salted boiling water until soft. Drain and
   set aside.
2 Heat the oil in a heavy-based pan and add the rice, stirring to coat
   it well with oil. Stir in the curry paste, if using, followed by the
   fish. Turn the rice and fish together as they warm in the pan.
3 When the mixture is well warmed through, stir in the butter and
   cream. Sprinkle the parsley and chopped egg over the kedgeree
   and serve.

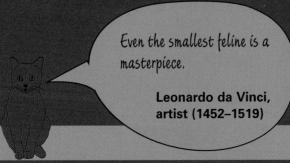

Even the smallest feline is a
masterpiece.

**Leonardo da Vinci,
artist (1452–1519)**

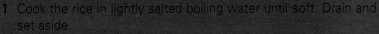

cartoon cats

On paper, cartoon cats have been around since 1914, when *Rainbow*, a children's comic with a lively 'Rainbow Cats Colony', was published. Since then there have been the strip-cartoon cat, Heathcliff, an anti-hero of a cat, named after the hero of Emily Bronte's *Wuthering Heights*, and modelled, according to his creator, on Humphrey Bogart; Garfield, an irrepressible, disreputable cat who began appearing in newspapers in the 1980s; and the cartoon cats of such artists as Bernard Kliban, Saul Steinberg, Siné and Ronald Searle.

The first film cartoon cat was Krazy Kat, who moved from Hearst newspapers to the silent screen in 1916. The first feline movie super star was Felix the Cat: in his heyday in the 1920s he was more popular than Charlie Chaplin or Buster Keaton. Tom and Jerry, the greatest cat-and-mouse movie cartoon duo, were created for MGM in the 1930s and went on to win seven Oscars and to star with such Hollywood greats as Gene Kelly and Esther Williams. After them came the lisping Sylvester, who never quite caught the canary; Walt Disney's *Aristocats*; television's laid-back and streetwise Top Cat, and many more ...

loafing around

This is a family-sized meatloaf. For two or three meals just for your cat, halve the ingredients.

500 g/1 lb finely minced beef
25 g/1 oz/½ cup fresh breadcrumbs
½ small onion, chopped
1 garlic clove, chopped
¼ teaspoon ground mace
2 tablespoons chopped fresh herbs
  (such as parsley, thyme, basil)
4–8 tablespoons milk or water
salt and freshly ground black pepper

1 Mix all the ingredients together, adding the liquid in spoonfuls, until the mixture is smooth and moist but easy to handle.
2 Shape into a loaf and stand it on a lightly oiled baking sheet. Place a piece of greaseproof paper on top. Bake in a preheated oven, 190°C/375°F/Gas Mark 5, for about 45 minutes.
3 Serve adults slices of meatloaf, with a meat gravy or a tomato sauce. Give your cat a slice broken up into bite-sized pieces, with a little gravy, if liked.

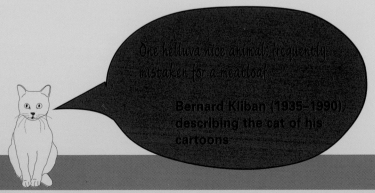

One helluva nice animal, frequently mistaken for a meatloaf.

Bernard Kliban (1935–1990), describing the cat of his cartoons

9-lives liver mousse

This is an easy recipe which can be made with fresh or frozen chicken livers. The basic recipe requires half the quantity of butter to chicken livers, plus a flavouring and herb. No extra salt is needed.

250 g/8 oz chicken livers, defrosted if frozen
125 g/4 oz butter
1 garlic clove, crushed or 1 teaspoon brewer's yeast
pinch of dried thyme or oregano
toast, to serve, optional

1 Trim the chicken livers, removing the cores.
2 Melt about 25 g/1 oz/2 tablespoons of the butter in a heavy-based saucepan and add the chicken livers. Cook them, turning, for 2 to 3 minutes. Add the garlic or brewer's yeast and the herb and continue cooking for a few minutes more. The chicken livers should be still a little pink inside.
3 Transfer the chicken livers to a blender or food processor and add the remaining butter. Process to a smooth purée.
4 Serve the mousse spread on bite-sized pieces of toast, if liked.

32

cat stars

Jinxie, a handsome Himalayan, helped bring off some of the best jokes in 'Meet The Parents' (2000).

the cat got the crème

This recipe for crème brûlée
is enough to feed four humans
and one cat, and is especially
good for a cat that is
particularly finicky or
recovering from illness.

300 ml/½ pint/1¼ cups single cream
300 ml/½ pint/1¼ cups double cream
5 large egg yolks, lightly beaten
½ teaspoon vanilla extract
25 g/1 oz granulated sugar
4 teaspoons demerara sugar

1 Bring the two creams to boiling point in a heavy-based saucepan,
   but do not let the mixture boil.
2 Transfer the cream to a bowl over a saucepan of simmering water.
   Stir in the beaten egg yolks, vanilla extract and sugar. Cook,
   stirring, until the mixture thickens and coats the back of a spoon.
3 Divide the mixture among five ramekin dishes (one of them is for
   your cat). Serve the cat's mixture when it has cooled to warm-on-
   the-tongue temperature. Cool the four remaining ramekins in the
   fridge. When they are chilled, sprinkle demerara sugar over each
   and put them under a hot grill until the sugar has caramelized.

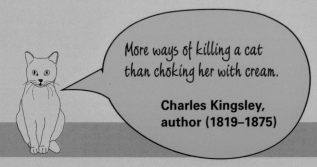

More ways of killing a cat
than choking her with cream.

**Charles Kingsley,
author (1819–1875)**

musical cats

- Cats have much better hearing than humans and a much wider auditory range. Experiments have shown that they can also discriminate finely between musical tones. French writer Théophile Gautier had a female cat, Madame Gautier, who did not care for the sound of a high A note sung by a woman. While Gautier accompanied women singers, the cat would sit quietly on the piano, putting out a paw to cover the mouth of any singer who hit that offending top A.
- Composer Henri Sauguet's cat, Cody, would become ecstatic when it heard the music of Debussy being played on the piano, leaping on the pianist's lap and licking his hands as he played.
  - Maurice Ravel included in his one-act opera *L'Enfant et Les Sortilèges* a very realistic cat duet for baritone and mezzo-soprano. The 'miaows' for the duet were provided by Colette, who wrote the opera's libretto in eight days.
  - Only in America ... When the All-American Glamour Kitz Contest, sponsored by Kitz Pan Litter, was held in 1974, one of the finalists was a piano-playing shaded silver Persian called Frazier.

34

tigger's teatime temptations

Cats enjoy sandwiches, provided the bread is fresh and wholegrain and the fillings are tasty. Put just a smear of butter on the bread. Madame Gautier and Cody, happily relaxing on a sofa by the piano in their masters' drawing rooms, would leap to their feet for squares of sandwiches with these fillings.

- **Sardines:** Drain sardines canned in oil and mash them with cream cheese or cottage cheese and chopped fresh parsley.
- **Ham:** Chop up a slice of ham and mix it into a spoonful of mayonnaise with some chopped fresh parsley or basil.
- **Pâté:** Fishy Wishes on page 14 makes a great sandwich spread, as does a shop-bought kipper pâté, enlivened with a sprinkling of brewer's yeast and some chopped fresh parsley.
- **Potted shrimps:** Mix the shrimps with a little cottage cheese and finely chopped lettuce.

You haven't lived until you have lived with a cat.

Doris Day, film actress and singer (b.1924)

Pussy cat, pussy cat, where have you been?
I've been to London to look at the queen.
Pussy cat, pussy cat, what did you there?
I frightened a little mouse under her chair.

Traditional nursery rhyme (the queen was Elizabeth I of England)

36 first cats

There have been many cats in the White House.

- Among Theodore Roosevelt's cats were Slippers, and Tom Quartz, whose biography was published.
- Calvin Coolidge had four cats, including Timmy, who would let the President's pet canary sit between his paws.
- Tom Kitten belonged to John F. Kennedy's daughter, Caroline.
- Gerald Ford's daughter, Susan, had a Siamese called Shan.
- The Siamese belonging to Jimmy Carter's daughter, Amy, answered to Misty Malarky Yin Yang.
- A multi-million dollar industry grew up around Bill Clinton's cat, Socks, who received so much mail at the White House that he was given his own letterbox.

caviar for aristocats

Perhaps you've won the lottery and wish your cat to share in your wealth? Here are the ingredients for the perfect food treat, courtesy of Tsar Nicholas I of Russia, who fed it to his cat Vashka. Quantities are to your cat's taste.

best Beluga caviar
vintage champagne
French dormouse,
   finely minced
unsalted butter
woodcock's egg,
   lightly beaten
cream
hare's blood

1 Poach the caviar in enough champagne to cover it.
2 Drain the caviar and put it in a bowl with the remaining ingredients. Mix well together, adding more cream and hare's blood as necessary to make a fairly soft, but not liquid, mixture.

super salescats

Two pairs of cats, on either side of the Atlantic, have achieved great fame selling cat food on television.

First on screen was Arthur, a handsome white cat skilled at scooping food out of a can with his paw. He appeared on British television in 309 commercials between 1966 and 1975, sending sales of the cat foods produced by his owners, Spillers, rocketing. Ten years after Arthur had died, at the good age of nearly 17, a replacement for him was found in an animal shelter in London. Arthur II was also large and white and pretty good at hitching food out of a can with his paw.

Across the Atlantic, a big ginger tom, rescued from a Chicago animal shelter in 1968, also spent ten years advertising cat food on television. This was Morris, a cat so famous that he appeared on TV chat shows, visited the White House and starred in a movie. He won a Patsy, the animal equivalent of an Oscar, in 1973. When he died in 1978, he was replaced by Morris II who also had a brilliant career, including campaigning to be chosen as a candidate for the Presidency of the United States.

38

rascal's risotto

A recipe for television stars
and other sophisticats.

3–4 chicken livers, cores removed
2 teaspoons sunflower oil
½ garlic clove, crushed
2 tablespoons tomato juice
25 g/1 oz/¼ cup cooked rice

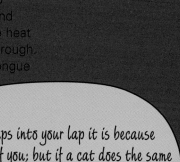

1 Cut the chicken livers into quarters.
  Put the oil and garlic in a heavy-based
  saucepan and heat to moderately hot.
  Add the pieces of chicken liver and stir-
  fry them until they are lightly cooked.
2 Add the tomato juice, stirring it into
  the mixture. Add the cooked rice and
  continue to stir-fry over a moderate heat
  until the mixture is well warmed through.
3 Cool the mixture to warm-on-the-tongue
  temperature and serve.

If a dog jumps into your lap it is because
he is fond of you; but if a cat does the same
thing it is because your lap is warmer.

**Alfred North Whitehead,
British philosopher
(1861–1947)**

nine lives and counting

Two cats share the record for long lives. Female tabby Ma, from Devon, England, and champion show cat Grandpa Rex Allen, from the USA, were both 34 when they died, Ma in 1957 and Grandpa Rex Allen in 1998.

The two hold the record because the birth date of tabby tom Puss, also from Devon, could not be confirmed, but he was thought to have had his 36th birthday the day before he died in 1939.

There must be something special about the air of southern England because Spike, who was Britain's oldest cat when he died at 31 in 2001, came from Dorset, one county along the coast from Devon. Spike's owner put his great age down to a daily dose of aloe vera.

seven-year scratch

The accepted way of comparing a cat's age with that of humans is to multiply the cat's years by seven. Some experts think that once a cat is nearing feline old age, multiplying its years by ten gives a truer comparison.

groomin' marvellous

Roll back your cat's years with
this nutrition-packed, lively-on-
the-tongue recipe.

125 g/4 oz sardines or pilchards canned
  in tomato sauce
1–2 tablespoons mashed hard-boiled egg
1 tablespoon chopped cooked spinach
2 teaspoons plain yogurt
1 tablespoon cooked rice (brown rice is
  best for fibre)
¼ teaspoon brewer's yeast

1 Put all the ingredients in a bowl and mix
   well together.

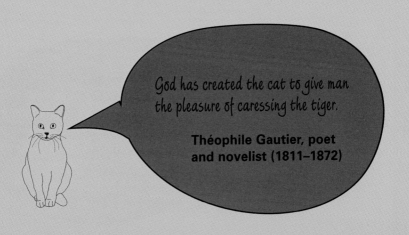

God has created the cat to give man
the pleasure of caressing the tiger.

**Théophile Gautier, poet
and novelist (1811–1872)**

stalker's salmon dream

This is the moggy version of the aristocratic fare Tsar Nicholas I fed his Vashka (see page 37) – just as delicious and within ordinary mortals' price range. Fish roe (for example lumpfish roe) can be found in jars on supermarket deli shelves. Herring would make a good substitute for the smoked salmon.

1 tablespoon chopped smoked salmon
1 teaspoon black or red fish roe
1 teaspoon soured cream or crème fraîche
a little finely chopped fresh parsley

1 Mix all the ingredients together and serve at once.

What female heart can gold despise?
What cat's averse to fish?

Thomas Gray, English poet (1716–1771) in 'Ode on the Death of a Favourite Cat'

42

tummy-tickling treats

Although really sugary foods such
as chocolates are not a good
thing to give your cat, other
treats may be much appreciated.
For example:

- **Bite-sized cubes of hard cheese and apple.**
- **Cubes of avocado** (with or without an oily
dressing).
- **Segments of tangerine or satsuma.**
- **Sweet seedless grapes.**
- **Beef-flavoured crisps.**
- **Yeast extract-flavoured pretzels.**
- **Catnip (*Nepata cataria*).** Also called catmint,
this herb is powerfully attractive to cats, because
of a chemical called nepetalactone it contains.
Grow it in the garden so your cat can roll in it or
buy or make toys stuffed with it (see page 26)
for your cat to wrestle with.

posh nosh

Contrary to experts' advice, the favourite
breakfast of Ernest Hemingway's cat
Boise, his best friend in Cuba, was chilled
mango slices. For dinner, Boise liked
halves of alligator pear (aguacate) filled
with an oil and vinegar dressing.

fat cats

The record for the heaviest domestic cat in the world has long been held by an Australian neutered tabby called Himmy. At his greatest, Himmy weighed 21.3 kg (46 lb 15¼ oz). His measurements included 38 cm (15 inches) around the neck and 84 cm (33 inches) around his middle. He died, aged ten, in 1986.

Tom, a neutered male living in New York, weighed slightly less than Himmy, but had a greater girth, being 91 cm (36 inches) around his middle. Tom was 17 when his owner told *The Guinness Book of Records* about him in 1980.

The heaviest British cat was a male tabby called Poppa, from Wales. In 1984, when he was 11, he weighed in at 20.2 kg (44½ lb). His owner put him on a diet shortly after, perhaps because the daily food bill was so high: one and a half cans of cat food, one can of evaporated milk, two handfuls of cat biscuits, a selection of potatoes, carrots, cabbage and gravy, and some home-made sponge cake!

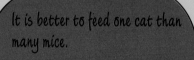

It is better to feed one cat than many mice.

Norwegian proverb

slimline rabbit stew

Cats like all game, probably because it retains more of the scent of the wild than other meats. It is also lean and high in protein.

2 teaspoons flour
2 teaspoons bonemeal
pinch of salt
250 g/8 oz boneless rabbit meat, cubed
oil, for stir-frying
1 garlic clove, crushed
125 ml/4 fl oz/½ cup chicken stock
1 tablespoon tomato juice
1 teaspoon chopped fresh parsley

1 Mix together the flour, bonemeal and salt. Toss the rabbit meat in the mixture to coat it.
2 Heat the oil in a heavy-based frying pan. Add the garlic and cook it briefly. Add the rabbit and brown it on all sides. Remove the rabbit pieces from the pan and put them in an ovenproof casserole.
3 Pour the stock and tomato juice into the pan, with any leftover flour mixture. Stir well, scraping up the pan juices and cooking gently until the stock reaches boiling point. Add the parsley, stir, and pour the sauce over the rabbit in the casserole.
4 Cover the casserole and cook in a preheated oven, 180°C/350°F/ Gas Mark 4 for 1 hour.

cats in literature

Cats have been inspiring literature ever since *Aesop's Fables* were written in the sixth century BC. A couple of centuries later cats were appearing in bestiaries, written first in Greek, then in Latin. Soon, cats had become accepted as the perfect companions for solitary writers.

By the 17th century the French writer La Fontaine could write that the intelligence of cats could be placed above that of dogs and uncomfortably close to humans. Three centuries after him, Nobel Prize-winning writer Ernest Hemingway summed up the reason for his great love of cats: 'The cat has complete emotional honesty – an attribute not often found in humans.'

It is not surprising, then, that so many cats, having found their way into writers' hearts, should also have found their way into literature.

If you want to write, keep cats.

Aldous Huxley, novelist (1894–1963)

hodge's oyster casserole

Samuel Johnson's 'very fine cat'
Hodge loved oysters. The great
man would buy the oysters
himself, lest the servants, sent
shopping for a cat, would take
against Hodge.

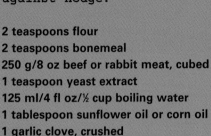

2 teaspoons flour
2 teaspoons bonemeal
250 g/8 oz beef or rabbit meat, cubed
1 teaspoon yeast extract
125 ml/4 fl oz/½ cup boiling water
1 tablespoon sunflower oil or corn oil
1 garlic clove, crushed
4–5 oysters

1 Mix the flour and bonemeal together. Toss
   the meat in the mixture to coat. Put the
   yeast extract in a mug and pour in the
   boiling water. Stir to mix and set aside.
2 Heat the oil in a flameproof casserole.
   Add the garlic and cook it briefly. Add
   the floured cubes of meat and cook for
   1–2 minutes so that the flour takes up the
   fat. Pour in the yeast extract mixture and
   stir it in. Add the oysters.
3 Cover the casserole, and cook in a
   preheated oven, 150–160°C/300–325°F/
   Gas Mark 2–3, for about 2 hours.

kitten's first feast

Kittens are best fed on their mother's milk, but it is good to start introducing something more solid after the first few weeks of life. Here are two cereal mixtures that kittens really enjoy. Offer them just once or twice a week at first.

for gruel:

1 tablespoon fine oatmeal
600 ml/1 pint/2½ cups milk

1 Mix the oatmeal to a paste with 2–3 tablespoons of the milk. Bring the remaining milk nearly to the boil and stir in the oatmeal paste. Cook for about 10 minutes, stirring occasionally, without letting the mixture boil.

for porridge:

organic porridge oats, cooked according to packet instructions
goat's milk yogurt

1 Give kittens a small amount of porridge, with a little goat's milk yogurt stirred in.

Now, Dinah, tell me the truth, did you ever eat a bat?

Alice, as she falls down the rabbit hole in Lewis Carroll's *Alice's Adventures in Wonderland* (1865)

kitten tales

In literature, kittens often come in threes. There are Beth March's three kittens that Jo took to cheer up the sick boy next door in Louisa May Alcott's *Little Women*; Tom Kitten, Mittens and Moppet behaving badly in Beatrix Potter's *The Tale of Tom Kitten*; and Orlando the Marmalade Cat's three children, Pansy, Blanche and Tinkle.

We are not sure how many kittens Don Marquis's mehitabel had. Archy, the literate cockroach typing out mehitabel's story without punctuation or capital letters because he was not heavy enough to work the shift key, mentioned the alley cat's lively kittens often during the many years their story appeared in newspaper columns and in his books.

Lewis Carroll gave his heroine, Alice, a cat called Dinah, who had two kittens, a black one called Kitty and a white one called Snowdrop. Both kittens had important parts to play in *Through the Looking-Glass*.

salmon supper

Buy salmon fillet rather than
salmon steaks for this dish and
you will have few, if any, bones
to remove.

about 125 g/4 oz piece of fresh salmon
small knob of butter
1 teaspoon chopped chives
pinch of salt

1 Set the salmon on a square of foil. Put the butter on the
salmon and sprinkle over the chives and a little salt. Pull up the
sides of the foil and make a well-sealed parcel. Put the parcel
in an ovenproof dish.

2 Cook in a preheated oven, 180°C/350°F/Gas Mark 4, for
15–20 minutes. Carefully unwrap the parcel, so that none of
the juices are lost. Lift out the salmon and flake it, removing
any bones. Break the skin into pieces and add it to the flaked
fish. Pour over the parcel juices to moisten. Serve the fish
when it has cooled to warm-on-the-
tongue temperature.

There is no doubt that it is very
flattering when a cat jumps on to
your lap.

Kingsley Amis, novelist
(1922–1995)

sarah snow's whiting

This is an elegant fish dish, its touch of green matching Sarah Snow's eyes. If you find that too much milk disagrees with your cat, use goat's milk instead of cow's milk.

125 g/4 oz piece of whiting or other white
  fish fillet
350 ml/12 fl oz/1½ cups milk
1 teaspoon chopped chives
25 g/1 oz cooked green peas
25 g/1 oz cooked rice

1 Put the fish, milk and chives in an ovenproof dish. Cover and bake in a preheated oven, 180°C/350°F/Gas Mark 4, for about 20 minutes.
2 Lift the fish fillet out of the milk and flake it, discarding any bones. Mix the fish with the peas and rice, moistening the mixture to your cat's liking with the milk. (Keep any remaining milk for another meal for your cat, perhaps with some more rice or dry cat food added.)

guiding paws

sarah snow

The cat that kept Kingsley Amis company as he wrote was a long-haired, green-eyed, white cat called Sarah Snow.

classic cats

🐾 **Puss-in-Boots**, the invention of 17th century French writer Charles Perrault, is a clever and sophisticated cat whose exploits turn a low-born youth into a nobleman fit to marry a princess. The story's theatrical quality made it perfect for turning into pantomime, the form in which Puss-in-Boots is best known today.

🐾 **The Cheshire Cat**, with a wide grin that remains in the air after the cat has vanished, is the most memorable of the animals encountered by Alice in Lewis Carroll's *Alice's Adventures in Wonderland*.

🐾 **'The Cat that Walked by Himself'** is one of Rudyard Kipling's best-loved *Just So Stories*. The story explains why Man cannot quite tame the Cat: 'He will kill mice, and he will be kind to babies ... But when he has done that, and between times, and when the moon gets up and the night comes, he is the Cat that walks by himself, and all places are alike to him.'

🐾 **Mehitabel**, an alley cat who is 'toujours gai' and shouts an insouciant 'wotthehell' at her world and its problems, was the invention of New York columnist Don Marquis. The adventures of 'archy and mehitabel' were published in newspaper columns for many years, and were sold in book form from the late 1920s.

Orlando the Marmalade Cat, his wife Grace and three children, have entranced several generations of children in books written and illustrated by Kathleen Hale between 1938 and 1972.

The Cat in the Hat, created by Dr Seuss (Theodor Seuss Giesel), began teaching small children to read in the 1950s. Dr Seuss's books, with their comicbook tone and often violent humour, broke new ground in children's cat books.

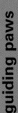
guiding paws

the master's cat

Charles Dickens kept one of the kittens born to his cat Williamina. The female kitten, called the Master's Cat, grew up with a mind of her own. She would sit on Dickens's desk while he was working and, if she thought it was late, would snuff out the candle with her paw.

cat burg-lars

This quick-to-make treat uses cooked chicken, but works equally well with turkey.

4–5 tablespoons minced chicken meat, cooked
1 garlic clove, crushed
2 teaspoons plain yogurt
1 small egg, lightly beaten
2 tablespoons fresh breadcrumbs
leaves stripped off 2 sprigs of thyme or
**   marjoram**
1–2 spinach or cabbage leaves, chopped
a little salt
olive oil, for frying

1 Mix together the chicken, garlic, yogurt, egg and breadcrumbs. Stir in the herb, greens and salt. Divide the mixture in half and shape into two burgers. Put in the fridge for 10–20 minutes.

2 Heat the olive oil to hot in a heavy-based frying pan, add the burgers and brown over a high heat on both sides. Reduce the heat and cook, turning once, for 6–8 minutes, until cooked through.

3 Pour a little water into the pan and scrape up the juices to make a thin sauce. Serve the burgers cooled and broken into pieces, with the sauce poured over.

tomcat tartare

Really fresh minced beef is just about the only meat that can safely be served raw to cats. There are likely to be bacteria and enzymes in all other raw meats and fish that could be harmful to cats, but which are destroyed by cooking. This tangy variation on the classic raw steak dish is particularly appealing to cats.

3 tablespoons minced steak
1 egg yolk
2 anchovy fillets in oil (not brine), drained and chopped
parsley, to garnish (optional)

1 Mix together the steak and egg yolk and sprinkle the pieces of anchovy fillet on top. Serve at room temperature, sprinkled with parsley if liked.

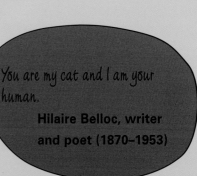

You are my cat and I am your human.

Hilaire Belloc, writer and poet (1870–1953)

choosing cats

Most of us choose alley cats – cats of very mixed parentage – for pets. But for many cat fanciers, the only cat to have is a pedigree, that is, one from a recognized breed.

The selective breeding of cats has been a serious business only since the end of the 19th century. In the comparatively short time since, hundreds of breeds and varieties of pedigree cat have been created, most of them with clubs and societies devoted to preserving and promoting their unique characteristics.

56

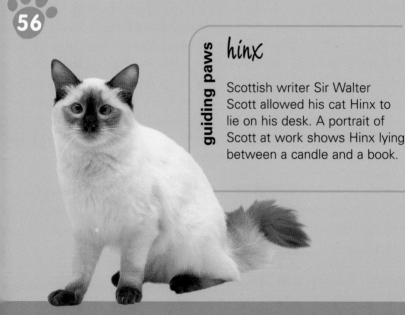

guiding paws

hinx

Scottish writer Sir Walter Scott allowed his cat Hinx to lie on his desk. A portrait of Scott at work shows Hinx lying between a candle and a book.

cool cat crunchy crumbs

Cats like home-made bites with
crunch, either on their own as
a snack or sprinkled over other
food. Here are two crisp treats.

for yeast crunchies:

**wholemeal bread crusts, cut into
bite-sized pieces
beef or yeast extract, dissolved in hot water**

1 Brush the pieces of crust on all sides with enough of the beef
or yeast mixture to moisten the bread without making it soggy.
2 Spread the pieces of bread on a baking sheet and bake on the
lowest shelf of a preheated oven, 140°C/275°F/Gas Mark 1,
until dried. Cool and store in an airtight container.

for cat's crumbs:

**3 slices of wholemeal bread, crumbed
2 teaspoons garlic flakes, or chopped garlic
lightly fried in a little oil**

1 Spread the breadcrumbs on a baking sheet and sprinkle over
the garlic.
2 Bake in a preheated oven, 150°C/300°F/Gas Mark 2, for about
30 minutes, or until crisp.

shaping up

From the Abyssinian to the York Chocolate, the American Bobtail to the Urals Rex, there are nearly 100 basic pedigree cat breeds, plus many varieties. Start your search for your perfect cat by deciding what shape you prefer. There are only two:

• 'Cobby' with full, round eyes in a round head, large in relation to the short thick body on sturdy legs.

• Lean and svelte, typified by the Siamese and other Oriental cats, with a long, wedge-shaped head and almond eyes, and an elegantly thin body and limbs and a long, thin tail.

Next, you have to decide on the type and colour of hair:

• Hair is either long-haired or short-haired, although there are sub-groups with semi-long hair. The hair can be fine or thick, straight or curly.

• Choice of colour and pattern is bewilderingly vast. Encyclopedias list up to 60, from Agouti and Auburn to Van and White, with many imaginatively named colours in between.

• Whether long- or short-haired, cats can be further subdivided according to face shape, which can be round, intermediate-shaped, wedge-shaped or non-pedigree.

kitty omelette

Cooked eggs are nutrient-packed treats for cats – three a week being the optimum number to give them. A one-egg omelette makes a great base for many favourite foods – from flaked fish and minced chicken to herbs, vegetables and cheese.

1 egg
1–2 teaspoons milk
small knob of butter
2–3 teaspoons filling, such as cottage cheese, grated hard cheese, chopped cooked Brussels sprouts or broccoli, chopped cooked meat or fish, or chopped fresh herbs, or a mixture

1 Beat together the egg and milk lightly. Melt the butter in an omelette pan. Pour in the egg mixture and cook over a moderate heat until the egg has started to set.

2 Sprinkle over the chosen filling(s) and continue cooking until the egg is set, but not too dry. Fold the cooked omelette over and serve it cut into strips or bite-sized pieces.

> If you want to live long, be healthy and fat, drink like a dog and eat like a cat.
>
> **German proverb**

paws for pudding

While cats do not need the starchy carbohydrate in rice, the grain provides bulk and fibre and, as in this seafood rice pudding, helps make other, more expensive, ingredients go further.

50 g/2 oz/generous ¼ cup short-grain rice
600 ml/1 pint/2½ cups milk
50 g/2 oz cooked white fish, flaked
a few cooked prawns, roughly chopped
2 teaspoons chopped fresh parsley
pinch of salt

1 Put all the ingredients in a lightly greased baking dish and cover with foil.
2 Bake in a preheated oven, 150°C/300°F/Gas Mark 2, for 2–2½ hours. The pudding should be deliciously creamy. Any leftovers may be kept in the fridge for a day and warmed up.

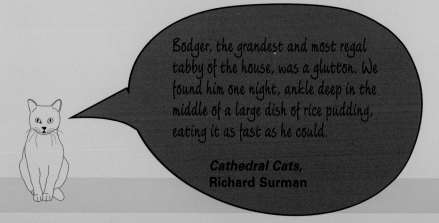

Bodger, the grandest and most regal tabby of the house, was a glutton. We found him one night, ankle deep in the middle of a large dish of rice pudding, eating it as fast as he could.

Cathedral Cats,
Richard Surman

quirky cats

• **Strange tails:** The American Bobtail has a stubby tail that stops above the hock. The Japanese Bobtail has a short pompon tail that can be either straight or curly. The basic Manx cat is tailless, but there are varieties with stubby and short tails (see page 8).

• **Curly hair:** The Devon and Cornish Rex both have hair that seems permed or crimped and there are no long guard hairs. The Cornish Rex's coat is curly, whereas the Devon Rex's is wavy. The La Perm appeared as a Rex mutation in the USA in the early 1980s; its hair is wonderfully soft and curly. The coat of the Selkirk Rex, another very recent breed with the Rex mutation, is soft and falls in individual curls.

• **Funny ears:** The only cat – so far – with folded-over ears is the Scottish Fold. This handsome cat with its ears folded forward can be traced back to a farm cat born in Scotland in 1961.

cat stars

Tonto was the companion of elderly New York widower, Harry, in his journey across America to make a new home in California in 'Harry and Tonto' (1974).

popularity stakes winners

- The world's most popular cat is the ordinary alley cat. They outnumber pedigree cats by more than ten to one. In some countries the cat population is 98 per cent ordinary or mongrel.

- Top of the list of registration records at the Cat Fanciers' Association (CFA), one of the world's largest cat registration organizations, is the Persian, or Longhair. This beautiful cat with thick, long hair and shortened face was bred in Great Britain from long-haired cats brought to Europe from the Middle East.

- The next most popular pedigree cat is the slim, svelte sapphire-blue-eyed Siamese, which came to the West from Thailand, where they were household and temple cats, in the 19th century. Examples of the breed appeared at the first-ever cat show in London in 1871.

- The Abyssinian has been moving rapidly up the registration listings, especially in the USA, in recent years. This short-haired cat with the striking 'ticked' coat pattern, was brought to the West from Abyssinia (now Ethiopia) in the 19th century.

Dogs have owners, cats have staff.

Anon

pussycat pasta

While the street cats of Italy
are expert at eating spaghetti,
non-Italian cats cope more easily
with pasta shapes!

2 teaspoons sunflower or olive oil
2 tablespoons minced beef
1 garlic clove, crushed
2 tablespoons canned chopped tomatoes
2 teaspoons brewer's yeast (optional)
pinch of salt
a little chopped parsley
cooked pasta shapes, to serve

1 Heat the oil in a heavy-based pan. Add
   the beef and garlic and cook, stirring, to
   brown the meat. Stir in the tomatoes,
   reduce the heat and simmer gently for
   10–12 minutes. Sprinkle over the brewer's
   yeast, if using, and salt and stir into the
   sauce. Stir in the parsley.
2 Serve the sauce spooned over cooked
   pasta shapes. Store any leftover sauce in
   the fridge.

index of recipes

acknowledgements

The Advertising Archive Ltd 38
Octopus Publishing Group Ltd /Jane Burton front cover top left, 40, 48, 52 /Stephen Conroy back cover top left, 11, 14, 18, 20, 22, 25, 26, 29, 31, 33, 35, 39, 41, 42, 45, 50, 54, 55, 56, 59, 60, 63 top /Steve Gorton back cover top right, 2, 34, 63 bottom, 64 /Ray Moller back cover bottom right, 7, 8, 10, 12, 24, 27, 37, 46 /Jerry Tubby front cover top right
Kobal Collection /Paramount 21
N.H.P.A. /Yves Lanceau 15
The Ronald Grant Archive /Hanna Barbera 30

The extract on page 60 is reproduced by kind permission of HarperCollins Publishers Ltd © Richard Surman 1997

Executive Editor: Sarah Ford
Editor: Sharon Ashman
Senior Designer: Joanna Bennett
Designer: Geoff Borin
Picture Research: Zoë Holtermann and Liz Fowler
Production Controller: Lucy Woodhead
Special photography: Stephen Conroy
Food Stylist: David Morgan

64